# Accidental Alphabet

Dianna Bonder

To my mom, the real Squirrelly Shirley.
Thank you for believing in me.

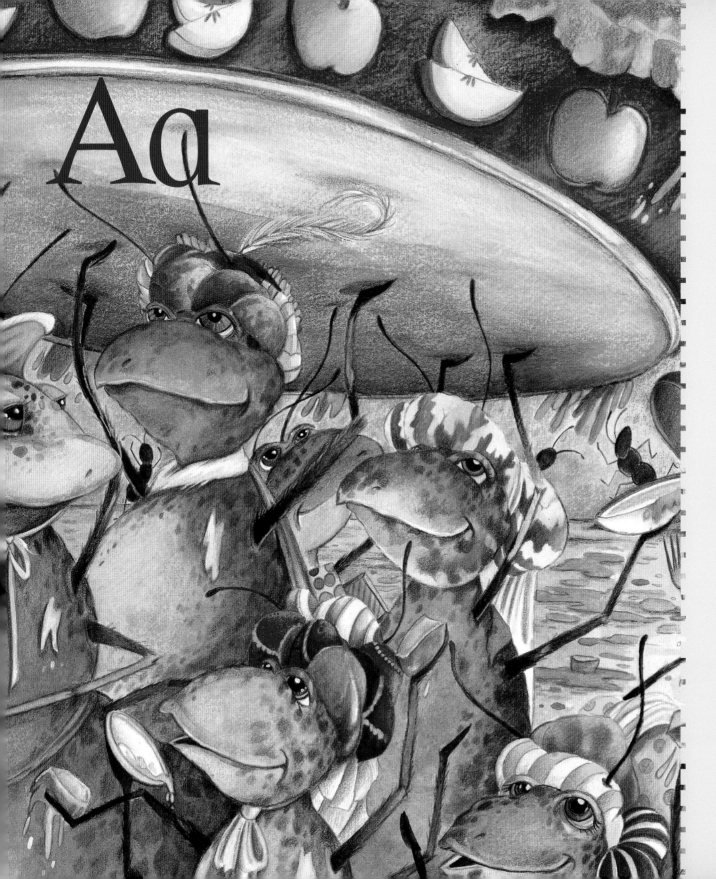

# Aa

Auntie Augusta had just
   baked a pie
with apples and allspice
   all stirred up inside.
She left it to cool,
   an aroma so sweet,
then an army of ants made
   their way up the street.

Advancing in order
   of age, weight, then size,
they scooped up the pie,
   right in front of her eyes.
Then marching in time
   with amazing ant skill,
they made their way back
   to their little ant hill.

As Beatrice baked her breakfast of bacon, eggs, and bread,
a bug bounced in her butter, and Beatrice turned beet-red.
"It seems I've ruined your breakfast," was the cheeky bug's rude boast,
and so with that, Bea scooped him out and spread him on her toast.

Clavin had a camel, who had a nasty cough.

      He coughed so much that Clavin feared he'd cough his humps right off!

So Clavin gave his camel a coughing-cure-cocktail.

      But Camel's cough continued, so he put him up for sale.

# Dd

Dilly danced the do-si-do,
with his dog,
who wore a bow.
Dancing fast, dancing slow,
Dilly fell and broke his toe.

# Ee

Edna Elway flipped an egg
as she prepared a cake.
Eleven egg flips in a row
and not a single break.
Then eighteen minutes
 later,
the egg fell to the floor,
and Edna's egg-flip record,
sadly, was no more.

Finkle Dinkle Fenheim
fried his fish in fat,
flipped it in a frying pan,
then fed it to his cat.

And when his cat
  was finished,
she rolled around the floor,
flicking Finkle with her tail
while meowing out
  for more.

Gg

Gertie grew a garden with guava, grapes, and greens,
golden-yellow grapefruit, and rows of jumping beans.
But then one day, her goat got loose, and gobbled up her crops,
and now her poor goat gets around with jumping-bean-like hops!

# Hh

Helen had a head of hair
piled high as it would go.
She held it with some
   hairpins
and tied it with a bow.

But Helen's hair was far
too thick and wouldn't stay
   in place.
The hairpins snapped,
   the bow fell out,
and hair flopped in
   her face.

Ii

Iggy the Iguana ate insects day and night.

Indulging in them by the pound gave Iggy great delight.

But Iggy soon felt icky, and ill in every way,

so Iggy cut his intake down to half a pound a day.

J j

Jiggle was a jester who loved to juggle jam,

jellybeans and jujubes, and cans of jellied ham.

But Jiggle had some trouble when he tried to jig and jump.

The jellied ham came crashing down and gave his head a lump.

King Kablonk was smitten
with a khaki-colored kitten.
Upon his knee,
    she meowed till three,
and then the king
    was bitten.

Len and the lazy llamas
      laid along the lawn.
Licking leaves and lima beans,
      they lounged from dusk till dawn.

Then Len and all the llamas
    leapt laps around their pen,
licked their lips and crossed their legs,
    and laid back down again.

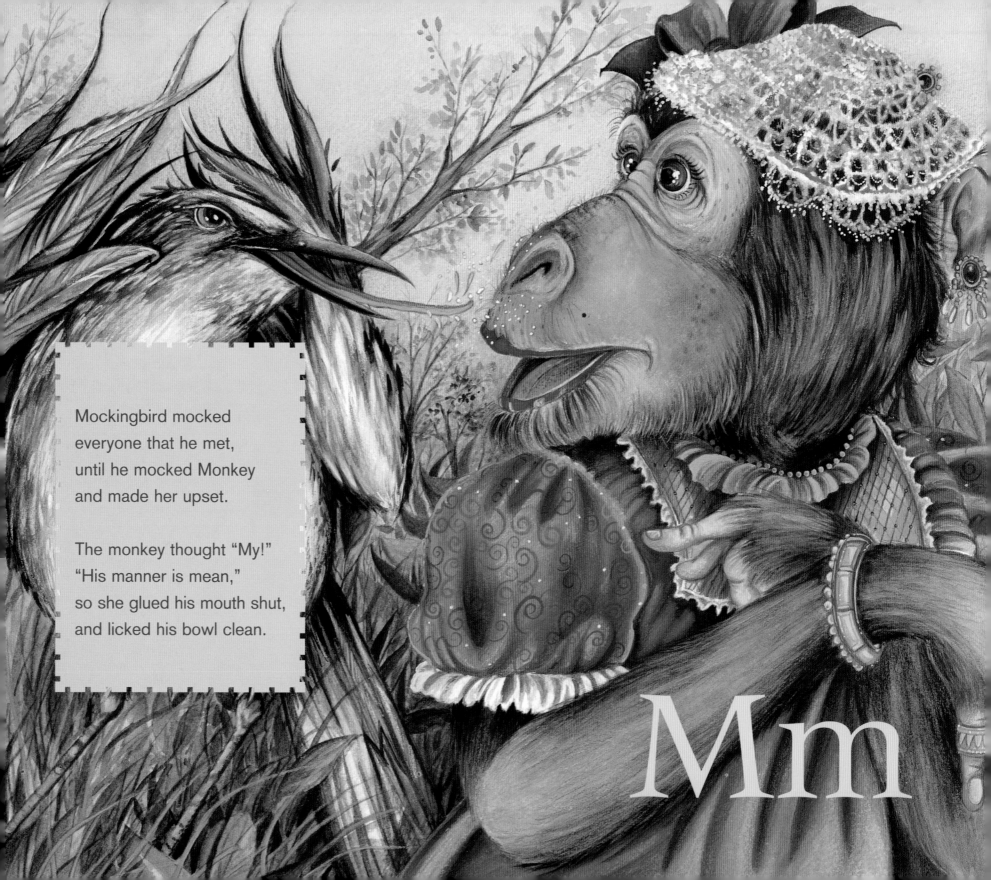

Mockingbird mocked
everyone that he met,
until he mocked Monkey
and made her upset.

The monkey thought "My!"
"His manner is mean,"
so she glued his mouth shut,
and licked his bowl clean.

Mm

# Nn

Nelly Newt napped,
and never took a break.
She napped at night,
she napped at noon,
she never stayed awake.

Nelly Newt napped,
and so did all her friends.
They napped all day,
they napped all week,
and then they napped
  weekends!

# Oo

Orville liked his olives—he ate them every day.

He ate them over onions, and often in soufflé.

He ordered them with oysters and just for a memento,

he took the oily oyster pearls and switched them with pimento.

Pp

Peggy liked her pizza with pickles and green peas,
seasoned with black pepper and topped with purple cheese.
But eating such a pizza is not exactly easy.
It gives poor Peg a purple hue and makes her tummy queasy.

Qq

Quinn quietly sat
on his little brown hat
when a quaint little quail
knocked him over.
The quail turned around,
and looked to the ground,
"My friend, you were
crushing my clover!"

There was a Rowdy Rooster, rambunctious as could be.
He'd rock and roll till morning, then rest till half past three.
And once that Rooster rested, he'd raise his ruffled head,
cock-a-doodle-dooing, until we went to bed.

Squirrelly Shirley
  spins around,
side to side, up and down.
She irons her sheets
  and mends her socks.
She never rests
  and always talks.

And sometimes when
  she tries to sleep,
she cannot stop
  her moving feet.
So Shirley simply lies
  in bed,
and lets her feet
  stay up instead.

Ss

Tt

Toad sat on the toadstool
drinking tepid tea,
and as a treat
    with tea that day,
he sprinkled in some flea.

Then sometime after
    ten o'clock,
Toad's tummy turned about.
It tumbled, rumbled,
    groaned, and moaned,
till he burped the flea
    back out.

# Uu

Ulf's underwear were ugly, uneven, and unfit,

undersized and full of holes, they'd pinch, and seams would split.

And though they were unsightly, Ulf wore them every day.

But when he took them off to wash, his undies ran away!

Vula Voo drank vinegar, it gave her vim and vigor,

and vegetables and vitamins helped her bones grow bigger.

But Vula drank a bit too much and soon outgrew her clothes.

And vinegar began to pour right out of Vula's nose.

Winston Walrus waddled by one windy afternoon.

He wore a watch that didn't work and whistled a warbly tune.

He walked toward a luncheon spot which seemed a wee bit quiet.

The window sign said "Closed all week" so Winston went on a diet.

Xavier Xay was excited one day
upon expecting his first x-ray.
     They examined his toes, then played x's and o's
          on top of Xavier's vertebrae.

Yikkity Yak, with his yellow backpack, yearned for yellow yams,
with Yorkshire pudding on the side, and yummy yucca jams.
But yews were all that ever grew throughout his small homestead,
so Yik cooked up some yew-tree stew and yucky yew-yeast bread.

Zoë loved her zebra, zig-zag stripes and all.

   She got him from the zoo one day when he was one inch tall.

Zebra had a zipper that zipped his heart up tight,

   and when they snuggled up in bed, his big heart warmed the night.

# Hints for finding hidden letters

A. Look for the ant wearing a red hat.

B. Look for a blue bow.

C. Look under the mouse.

D. Look under the dog.

E. Look beneath Edna's skirt

F. Look beside the cat's tail.

G. Look for the flower that isn't in the garden.

H. Look under a window.

I. Look beside the dragonfly.

J. Look for the green ribbons.

K. Look in the kitten's dish.

L. Look under a tree.

M. Look on the mockingbird's tail.

N. Look above the green newt's nose.

O. Look up on the hill of olives.

P. Look beside the pink striped patch.

Q. Look for the spilling water.

R. Look for the hen with the blue bonnet.

S. Look on the thread hanging from Shirley's hat.

T. Look beneath the clock.

U. Look under the underwear.

V. Look beside the doorway.

W. Look for the whistle.

X. Look on the collar.

Y. Look under the yak's tongue.

Z. Look above the blue bear.

# Can you find the answers?

A. How many ants are wearing hats?

B. What color is Beatrice's bow?

C. Can you find the thermometer?

D. What color is the dog's hat?

E. How many unbroken eggs can you see?

F. What is the cat's name?

G. How many jumping beans can you find?

H. How many hairpins are falling out of Helen's hair?

I. How many insects can you see?

J. Can you find the jellybeans?

K. How many toys does the kitten have?

L. How many llamas can you count?

M. How many pieces of jewelry is the monkey wearing?

N. How many newts are sleeping?

O. Which direction does Olive Ville point?

P. What kind of cheese is in the container?

Q. Can you find the four-leaf clover?

R. What time does the clock show?

S. Can you find the sewing needle?

T. What is the toad sprinkling on his tea?

U. Where is the tiny umbrella?

V. How many of Vula's buttons are popping off?

W. What is the name of the restaurant?

X. Who is winning the game of x's and o's?

Y. How many birds are on the yak's back?

Z. How many stuffed toys are on the bed?

# Answers

A. 5

B. Blue

C. In the camel's mouth

D. Red

E. 12

F. Felix

G. 13

H. 6

I. 11

J. Near the jester's hand and above his head

K. 5

L. 11

M. 5

N. 9

O. To the right

P. Parmesan

Q. The quail is carrying it

R. 1:30

S. In Shirley's hand

T. Fleas

U. On top of Ulf's hat

V. 5

W. Willy's Fish Restaurant

X. X is winning the game

Y. 4

Z. 5

Edited by Kathy Evans
Cover and interior design by Tanya Lloyd Kyi
Author photo by Cindy Kinash
Printed and bound in Hong Kong

NATIONAL LIBRARY OF CANADA CATALOGUING IN PUBLICATION DATA
Dianna Bonder, 1970–
    Accidental alphabet

    ISBN 1-55285-394-2

    1. English language—Alphabet—Juvenile literature.
2. Accidents—Pictorial works—Juvenile literature.  I. Title.
PE1155.B66 2002        j421'.1        C2002-910801-2

The publisher acknowledges the support of the Canada Council and the Cultural Services Branch of the Government of British Columbia in making this publication possible. We acknowledge the financial support of the Government of Canada through the Book Publishing Industry Development Program for our publishing activities.